ROCK STARS!

True Stories of Extreme Climbing Adventures!

Steve Bramucci

NATIONAL
GEOGRAPHIC

WASHINGTON, D.C.

NATIONAL GEOGRAPHIC and Yellow Border Design are trademarks of the National Geographic Society, used under license.

Since 1888, the National Geographic Society has funded more than 14,000 research, conservation, education, and storytelling projects around the world. National Geographic Partners distributes a portion of the funds it receives from your purchase to National Geographic Society to support programs including the conservation of animals and their habitats. To learn more, visit natgeo.com/info.

For more information, visit nationalgeographic.com, call 1-877-873-6846, or write to the following address:

National Geographic Partners, LLC
1145 17th Street NW
Washington, DC 20036-4688 U.S.A.

For librarians and teachers:
nationalgeographic.com/books/
librarians-and-educators

More for kids from National Geographic:
natgeokids.com

For rights or permissions inquiries, please contact National Geographic Books Subsidiary Rights: bookrights@natgeo.com

Designed by Ruth Ann Thompson

Library of Congress Cataloging-in-Publication Data

Names: Bramucci, Stephen, author.
Title: National geographic kids. Chapters : rock stars! / by Stephen Bramucci.
Other titles: Rock stars!
Description: Washington, DC : National Geographic Kids, [2018] | Series: National geographic kids. Chapters | Includes index.
Identifiers: LCCN 2017020446 | ISBN 9781426330490 (paperback) | ISBN 9781426330506 (hardcover)
Subjects: LCSH: Rock climbing--Juvenile literature.
Classification: LCC GV200.2 .B73 2018 | DDC 796.522/3--dc23
LC record available at https://lccn.loc.gov/2017020446

Printed in the United States of America
22/VP/2

Table of CONTENTS

A Climber's Vocabulary

ASCENT
The act of climbing up the face of a mountain or boulder

BETA
Advice gathered from other climbers on how to climb a specific route

CRUX
The hardest part of any climb

PITCH
A section of a climb usually about 160–200 feet (50–60 m)

PROJECT
When a climber works on a certain route for a long period of time, he or she calls it a project.

ROUTE
The path up a rock face that a climber follows during an ascent. Each rock face can have multiple routes to the top.

SEND
A slang word used by climbers that comes from the word "ascend." It means that a route was climbed successfully.

SUMMIT
The highest point on any mountain, rock face, or peak. It can also mean to reach the top of a climb.

Boulderers, like Ashima Shiraishi, climb large rocks as a sport.

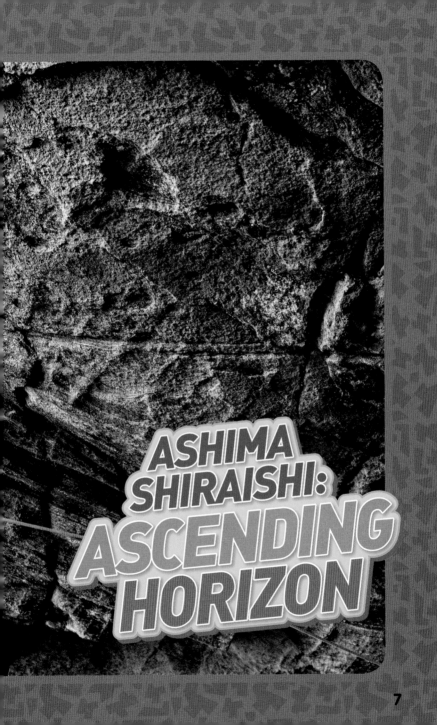

ASHIMA SHIRAISHI: ASCENDING HORIZON

Ashima Shiraishi began rock climbing at the young age of six.

Chapter 1

A RISING STAR

A week before her 15th birthday, Ashima Shiraishi (sounds like a-SHEEM-a shi-RAH-shee) hiked along a forest path on Mount Hiei (sounds like HEE-ay) in Japan. She drew the cool morning air into her lungs, passing tall pines and bright green bamboo groves. With each step, her excitement grew. She'd been waiting for this moment for months.

Ashima's father, who she calls Poppo, and her mentor, or adviser, Dai Koyamada (sounds like DIE koi-ah-MAH-dah), walked beside her up the mountain. Soon, they arrived at a massive, bean-shaped boulder named Horizon. The curved underside of the boulder creates a natural tunnel, nicknamed the "Red Cave." The roof of this cave is lined with ledges and handholds, which run along a crack in the limestone. These features form a "bouldering problem"—a climbing route low enough to the ground to be completed without ropes. It was this difficult problem that brought the trio (sounds like TREE-oh) to Japan.

Staring up at the Red Cave, Ashima drew a long breath and released it slowly. A few months earlier, Horizon had left her in tears. Now, she'd come back feeling like a more experienced climber. She'd been visualizing the route for months, practicing the skills she'd need to complete each move.

In order to finally send Horizon, Ashima knew she'd have to remain focused while keeping calm. This quality of stillness is a special gift all its own, one which Poppo Shiraishi, a dancer, knows very well.

"My dad tells me to have a quiet soul before I climb," Ashima said. "He talks about this state of nothingness—because if you're flustered and distracted, you won't be able to get to the top."

That serene (sounds like suh-REEN) attitude doesn't come overnight. It takes commitment and practice. To have that feeling of calm on Horizon, Ashima would need to pull together all of her experiences—every trick and skill she'd learned since first trying the sport of rock climbing.

Nine years earlier, as a six-year-old, Ashima's first climb was a scramble up Central Park's famous "Rat Rock" in New York City, where she lived. Her love of the sport grew quickly from there.

"I was really small so it was hard for me," she said, "but I fell in love with the movement of the sport and kept returning every single day."

Before long, Ashima began to enter competitions. She started beating adult climbers when she was only seven years old. It quickly became clear that this girl, who had grown up among high-rise buildings rather than mountain peaks, had a high "rock IQ." She understood the sport in a way few people do.

"You have to solve these puzzles," Ashima explained. "You learn to look at the problem and see yourself climbing before you've even started, and that's a real challenge."

Soon, Ashima was ready for harder climbs. When she was just eight, she mastered a tough bouldering problem called Power of Silence. The V Scale (see page 15) ranks bouldering problems from an easy V0 to a very hard V17. Power of Silence is rated a V10. By finishing such a hard route at such a young age, Ashima showed the climbing world that she was going to be a star!

When Ashima was only 10 years old, she climbed a V13 route called Crown of Aragorn. She was the youngest person on record to ever ascend that high of a bouldering grade. Soon, her shelves were lined with trophies, both for bouldering and for sport climbing (which is climbing with ropes and harnesses).

As she got older, Ashima's creativity wowed fans and fellow climbers. When she climbs, her smooth style often looks like a dance. Her body seems to naturally flow from one move to the next.

"It's hard to define flow in climbing," Ashima said, "because it's really the moment when your concentration and your breathing are in sync. You're climbing and your body is leading the way."

How Boulders Are Rated

V0

Bouldering problems are rated to tell other climbers how hard they are. The most common system is the Hueco Scale (sounds like WEH-co), or V Scale. This simple system rates problems from a V0 (the easiest problem) to a V17 (the hardest problem ever recorded).

V10+

The person who sends a route first gets to decide its rating. Dai Koyamada was the first to send Horizon, so he got to rate it.

Ashima climbs a boulder as her mentor Dai Koyamada spots her.

Chapter 2

THE FIRST TRIP TO HORIZON

While Ashima was competing in the United States, Dai Koyamada was testing out a "super project" he'd discovered in Japan. He called the boulder Horizon and began planning a climb that ran along the Red Cave's roof. Dai learned each move individually at first, and then practiced putting them together. His route was much longer than most bouldering problems, but that wasn't the only tricky part of the climb. In the hardest section, water slowly seeped through cracks in the cave's roof. This meant that the final holds were often wet and slick.

Dai struggled with Horizon for three years. Finally, he had a breakthrough. He'd been climbing the whole day. It wasn't until evening that he finished, completing the full 25-move ascent by lantern light. It was an exciting moment. He was the first to master the Red Cave.

He soon told another well-known boulderer about his success in Japan. He described the moves he'd needed to climb upside down along the cave's ceiling. The person he told? Ashima Shiraishi.

Ashima couldn't wait to tackle Horizon.

On her first trip to see the boulder, during her winter break from school, she felt struck by the beautiful setting. She was even more excited by the line, or possible route, along the Red Cave. She understood right away that it was going to be a challenge.

"Dai brought me to Japan because he knew I like to climb on cave ceilings," Ashima explained. "You feel like a spider or gecko, just dangling by your fingertips and your toes. But it takes a lot of core strength not to fall."

Soon, Ashima started to study Dai's beta—a series of moves used to help climb a route. She needed to master each piece one by one before tying the whole thing together. She caught on quickly, and the climb proved to be a natural fit for her skills. Still, it wasn't easy. As she practiced each move, her fingers grew raw and her muscles (sounds like MUSS-els) ached. Day after day, she kept trying, even when she was tired or frustrated.

Each morning, Ashima, Dai, and Poppo hiked to the boulder. Next, Ashima would lace up her climbing shoes and dust chalk on her hands. Then it was time to begin another day of trying to master the many difficult moves along the Red Cave's ceiling.

Soon, Ashima was ready to try putting all the moves together. This was where the hard work really began. Horizon's crux (sounds like KRUKS)—or hardest section of the climb—is very close to the end of the route. By the time Ashima got there,

she was exhausted.
Her fingers slipped,
her arms gave way, or
her footholds released.
Her mind was tired, too, from the long
hours of concentration (sounds like
con-sen-TRAY-shun).

Over and over, she tried and fell.
She wanted to send the problem so badly!
On the last day of her winter trip, she
gave the climb every bit of her effort.
She needed to complete her project before
returning to New York City.

When she got to the crux holds,
Ashima found that they were wet.
Her fingers slipped. She dropped safely
to the ground. She tried again. Again,
she fell. Tears welled up in her eyes.

What Is a Crux?

In climbing, the crux is the hardest part of the climb. It is the move or moves that are the most challenging. On longer climbs, there might be many cruxes. The crux on Horizon is the series of moves at the end. To get past it, Ashima would have to release her footholds and hang by her fingertips.

Sometimes, climbers talk about cruxes in real life, too! The hardest part of a test or a fight with a friend could end up being the crux of your day.

"I kept falling and falling on the last move," she said. "It was really frustrating. My fingers were bleeding and I cried."

With Poppo by her side, Ashima flew home. There were chores and schoolwork to do. Life moved on, but always, in the back of her mind, was Horizon. It had challenged her and pushed her to her very limit. But it hadn't broken her spirit.

Right away, Ashima started planning a return to Japan. Dai's super project had been passed down to her. Finishing Horizon was Ashima's goal now, and she put everything she had into preparing for her rematch with the rock.

Did You Know?

Mount Hiei, where Horizon is found, is most famous for a Buddhist monastery, which was built around A.D. 788.

Ashima climbs the ceiling of the Red Cave like a human spider.

Chapter 3

RETURN TO RED CAVE

Ashima was excited to head back to Japan to face Horizon again. But she was worried, too. She had put so much effort into preparing for this rematch. Would she be able to complete the route?

"I was pretty nervous," she said. "I know it's a common saying, but there had been blood, sweat, and tears put into that climb. I really beat myself down."

Ashima was putting a lot of stress on herself, but the people around her were there to help. Both Poppo and Dai would join her again on the trip. Her mom sewed brightly colored climbing pants for Ashima to wear each day. Even though she'd be alone on the boulder, she'd be reminded of the people who believed in her.

After a long flight, the day of Ashima's return to Mount Hiei finally arrived. The weather was chilly. It was perfect for climbing. As she walked toward Horizon, she saw bamboo shoots springing up from the soil. Everything was green and felt fresh. But there was one thing that both she and Dai knew might cause problems: There had been rain just a few days before. Too much water in the thin cracks along the route could make it slippery and even harder to climb.

Ashima began to climb. But just like before, her struggles with the crux continued. She fell over and over. Soon, her fingertips were raw and bleeding. Still, she kept trying.

Often times, climbers will take breaks between bouldering days to rest their bodies, but Ashima didn't want to waste time. For her, Horizon was the complete focus of the trip, and she wasn't about to slow down.

Two days had gone by without success (sounds like suck-SESS). On day three, she got ready for another try. A bit of water had seeped through the crack along the Red Cave. But everything else looked good. Ashima dusted her hands with powdered chalk. The chalk would keep them dry in the moist cracks. Then she pulled herself up onto the ceiling of the Red Cave.

Ashima's first moves followed the line of the crack. She used her feet almost like another pair of hands. She kept her breathing steady. She gripped each new handhold before moving her feet. With her body hanging upside down and her hands and feet moving her forward, Ashima really did look like a gecko!

"I feel like most beginners aren't aware of how important footwork is in climbing," she said. "It takes a lot of flexibility but allows your arms to recover."

Ashima moved along the roof quickly. It was all going smoothly. As she neared the crux, she came to a spot where she had to release both feet from the rock and swing her legs in front of her. She knew just what to do. Tightening (sounds like TITE-en-ing) her stomach muscles, she performed the move. She had to do it slowly. Too fast, and she'd swing herself off the rock!

As she swung her legs, Ashima felt excited. This was her chance! Some of the holds along the crack were wet, but she was in the flow. Finally, she neared the crux, where the cave roof curves away from the floor.

A Climbing Project

Climbing is more about dedication than getting something right on the first try. When climbers find a route that they want to spend their time and energy on, they call it a project. Dai Koyamada's super project—in which he became the first person ever to climb Horizon—took him three years to complete!

Between her trip to Japan in the winter and her return trip in the spring, Ashima's project had consumed her for three months. With hard work and commitment, she was able to use Dai's advice and her own skill to finally reach the top of Horizon.

"Right before I started the crux moves, I stopped for a second," she said. "To remind myself of exactly what I had to do."

Ashima's arms were wide apart, gripping the crimps—tiny rock ledges so narrow that she could only hold them with her fingertips—along the crack in the ceiling. From here, she had to release her feet completely, letting them hang down toward the ground. She'd need to use her stomach muscles again to control her body.

Did You Know?

When Poppo Shiraishi was a dancer, his wife, Ashima's mother, used to sew his costumes.

"Releasing your feet on such bad holds really makes you feel like you're going to let go," she said. "That's where you need the most core strength because you have to slow your body movement down when your feet kick out."

With every muscle in her body working together, Ashima brought her feet back up. She placed her left foot outside of her arms and slipped her right foot under her left arm. To get the right angle, she had to let her head drop lower toward the cave floor. With her toes biting into the rock, she released her left hand and turned sideways, heading toward the final and most difficult move.

Part of this last move was putting her fingers in a "finger lock"—a crack so small

Ashima could only fit two fingers. She crossed her arms to take hold of another crimp and let her feet off the rock a third time. She stretched her legs out into a split and felt with her feet for holds on the rock.

Down on the ground, Dai and Poppo cheered with excitement. The young bouldering star had completed the final part of the crux. From here, Ashima only had a few more moves before the wall curved upward. When she reached over her head and gripped a solid ledge, she knew she'd made it. She pulled herself up and scampered up to the top of the boulder.

She'd done it! She was the second person ever to climb Horizon, the first woman ever to climb such a difficult boulder, and the youngest person ever to ascend a V15. Ashima felt joy as she sat on top of the boulder, smiling down at Dai and Poppo. It was the best early birthday present in the world.

"Even after I fell down, I stood back up and tried again," Ashima said. "That's where all the joy comes from. Feeling like it was all really worth it."

Ashima's climb made news around the world. People who heard her story phoned and wrote letters to her, hoping to tell the story of her achievement (sounds like ah-CHEEV-ment). But what meant the most to the young climbing star was that she had tried hard and met her goal.

"That's why I climb," she said. The hard work that leads to the success is what makes her happy and keeps her climbing.

JIMMY CHIN:
THE QUEST FOR SHARK'S FIN

The climbing trio—Jimmy Chin,
Conrad Anker, and Renan Ozturk—
on Mount Meru.

Mount Meru, located in northeast India, is part of the Himalayan mountain range.

FAILURE AT 20,000 FEET

The sun was setting on Jimmy Chin and his expedition partners Conrad Anker and Renan Ozturk (sound like REE-naan OHZ-turk). They were 328 feet (100 m) from the summit of Mount Meru (sounds like MEE-roo) in the Garhwal Himalaya in India. They had to decide whether to push for the top or go back down. They'd been climbing for 17 days.

After being delayed for four days by a massive storm, they were so low on food that they'd resorted to eating cheese rinds, cooked over a propane fire. They were exhausted, and weeks of facing minus 20°F (–30°C) temperatures had left them without feeling in their fingers or toes.

The choice was clear. They had to turn back. If they tried to keep climbing, they'd be stuck sleeping on an exposed rock face without proper gear or food. It was too big of a risk to take.

"It's not easy turning around," Jimmy said, as the team began to descend toward their camp. If they kept going up, they knew they wouldn't make it.

Did You Know?

Besides being a famous climber, Jimmy Chin is a world-class photographer. His pictures have been on the cover of magazines like *National Geographic*!

Jimmy, Conrad, and Renan had been following a line called Shark's Fin, and it had proven to be just as dangerous as its name. The climb had demanded every ounce of their combined skill, experience, and bravery—and it had still been too much to handle.

As the trio headed down the mountain, Conrad was already thinking about his next attempt. He'd had his heart set on summiting Mount Meru ever since hearing about it from his mentor, Terrance "Mugs" Stump. Jimmy felt differently. In that moment—cold, hungry, and tired beyond the breaking point—he wouldn't even consider returning to Shark's Fin.

"I'm not coming back," he said. "Maybe it just wasn't meant to be climbed."

There was a good reason for Jimmy's fear. In more than 120 years of organized Himalayan climbing, Shark's Fin had *never* been summited. More than two dozen climbers had tried over the past 30 years, and every single one of them had failed—including Conrad himself just a few years earlier. In some cases it was the weather that defeated the climbers; other times it was a strategic mistake.

"Meru definitely had a reputation as an impossible climb," Jimmy said, remembering the first time he heard about the mountain. "The way Conrad brought up the trip, it was very nonchalant, and I think the more nonchalant Conrad is about suggesting a trip the more worried you ought to be."

As Jimmy and Renan discovered, the route was far more difficult than Conrad had let on. In fact, after the team's first attempt, other famous climbers tried to follow their path—only to fail in their efforts, too.

Jimmy came home from India in such bad shape that he had to use a wheelchair for his first three weeks off the mountain. But eventually his vow never to return to Shark's Fin softened. Renan also wanted to try again. With a new plan for how to approach the route, Conrad promised that things would be different the next time around.

As the team started to prepare for a return trip to Meru, disaster struck. Less than a year before the trip was set to depart, Renan suffered a serious accident while he and Jimmy were in Jackson, Wyoming, U.S.A., working on a video project. Renan took a bad fall while skiing down a dangerous slope—cracking his skull and breaking part of his neck, affecting blood flow to his brain.

After Renan's fall, doctors placed a special stent—a brace that helps open up blood flow—inside his head. Through many surgeries and a long road to recovery, he spoke eagerly about going back to Shark's Fin. To Jimmy and Conrad, this seemed impossible. But they hoped to keep their friend's spirits high. They did their best to hide their doubts.

"You don't have the heart to tell someone something's impossible," Jimmy said. "You're not going to at that moment say 'Dude, what are you talking about? You're never going back to Meru.' You just don't say those kind of things."

Jimmy's own time back in the United States wasn't easy either. Back in Wyoming's Teton Range, on the same project where Renan had been injured, a massive avalanche roared down the mountain while Jimmy was skiing down a slope.

"For a moment, it looks like slow motion," Jimmy said, "and the next moment everything went to fast-forward and I got swept away. I'm airborne, totally weightless."

The "Anti-Everest"

Meru is nicknamed the "anti-Everest." That's because Mount Everest—probably the most famous climb on Earth—can be summited by people who don't have years of technical climbing skill. The easier routes up Everest are more about endurance and how the body adjusts to having less oxygen at high altitudes.

Meru, however, is a very technical climb. It requires skills in a variety of climbing techniques. The big wall sections—the toughest, slowest parts of the climb—are at the very end of the route, when climbers are exhausted and low on food.

As a tidal wave of snow picked him up and spun him around, Jimmy tried to keep calm to preserve oxygen—just like a big wave surfer caught in the whitewash. The avalanche tumbled down 2,000 vertical feet (610 m). It tore up trees by the roots and broke loose huge blocks of ice and snow, carrying Jimmy along for a terrifying ride.

When the avalanche finally slowed, Jimmy was sure he'd be crushed under the weight of the snow. Instead, he felt a current below him, shoving his body toward the surface. During the avalanche, he'd assumed the worst, but now it seemed like he might survive. As the wave of snow finally came to a halt, Jimmy broke the surface—still buried up to his chest.

"I was like, I'm in one piece," he said. "I coughed up this huge chunk of snow and took this huge breath, and I looked at my arms … I couldn't even believe they were connected to my body."

Somehow, Jimmy hadn't been injured, but he was deeply shaken by the experience. He felt like he'd been given a second chance at life and really needed to think about how to move forward. Would he give up mountaineering? Did he want to risk another huge expedition? Did he still dream of summiting Meru?

In the end, Jimmy decided to be a part of Conrad's next big trip to Shark's Fin. Meanwhile, Renan had stuck to his word—he was training day and night while still wearing a neck brace and recovering from his injuries. His progress was incredible, but Jimmy and Conrad couldn't help but worry. What if the stent in Renan's skull failed to work in high altitudes or cold weather?

"We knew we had to trust him, to let him go," Jimmy said. "And that's what we did ... we trusted him."

It was settled. Jimmy, Conrad, and Renan would all make a second attempt on Meru together, as a team. They would believe in one another and be honest with each other if the climb proved too challenging.

Three years after their first summit attempt, the mountaineers headed back to India.

THE SUMMIT RIDGE

THE TEAM'S PREVIOUS END POINT

THE FIN PROPER

HOUSE OF CARDS

PORTALEDGE SNAPS

ALPINE RIDGE

RENAN BREAKS DOWN

This is the route Jimmy and crew had to conquer to summit Shark's Fin.

ADVANCE BASE CAMP

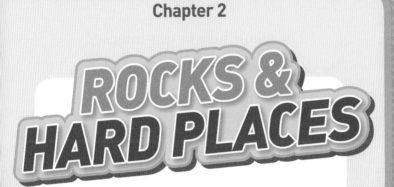

Chapter 2

ROCKS & HARD PLACES

For anyone hoping to climb Meru, the town of Gangotri, India, is literally the end of the road. This is where Jimmy, Conrad, and Renan began their second trip up Shark's Fin.

Before the serious climbing began, the team had to hike to the foot of the mountain and set up a base camp. As they hiked, Jimmy wondered if this really was the right choice.

"The whole hike in was intense," he said. "There's no doubt that I had a heavy heart going into it. It just felt like so much pressure."

The plan for this climb was different from the team's first attempt at Shark's Fin. They'd decided to take the first section—a steep incline of snow and ice—in one giant push. The goal was to get off the snow and make it to the nearly vertical rock face as quickly as possible.

During this stretch, which lasted 19 straight hours, Renan started acting strangely. His movements were slow, and his speech was slurred. His symptoms reminded Jimmy and Conrad of someone having a stroke. By the time the three climbers set up camp that night, Renan

had completely lost
the ability to speak.

Jimmy knew that
his friend was in
trouble. "He tried to
say something to me and it
was just complete gibberish. You
could see the alarm in his eyes that
however hard he was trying to speak,
it wasn't happening."

In their heads, Jimmy and Conrad
were already both coming to grips with
the idea of turning back. Maybe Renan's
condition was the result of his head injury
from the previous spring, the altitude, or
a combination of the two. The fact was,
it just didn't seem possible for him to
keep climbing. As they finally fell asleep,

Jimmy and Conrad knew their dream of summiting Meru was in danger of slipping away once again.

Jimmy awoke before Renan the next morning and watched his friend breathe out puffs of steam. The time had come to decide whether to head up Shark's Fin or begin their descent. Storms are a constant danger in the Himalaya, and spending too much time making a decision would only increase the risk of getting caught in one.

With their friend's life on the line, Jimmy and Conrad didn't want to make a mistake. As they started putting on their gear, Renan still couldn't form words, but he did seem more alert. Finally, he gave Jimmy a nod, as if to say: "I want to keep going."

Big wall climbing, like what Jimmy, Conrad, and Renan did on Meru, moves incredibly slowly. The climbers take turns setting a route, securing the ropes, organizing equipment, and hauling gear. In some cases, traveling 150 feet (46 m) might take a full day!

A portaledge is a platform, suspended with hooks and ropes, meant to create space for climbers to camp while hanging from a rock wall. These contraptions may look terrifying (see page 57), but they are a crucial part of big wall climbs all over the world.

After some help getting his equipment on, Renan actually led the next pitch. Jimmy and Conrad watched him closely, ready to turn around the second he got worse. To their surprise, the opposite happened— Renan seemed to get stronger as the day went on. He found a rhythm, and by nightfall he was able to speak again.

As the temperatures dropped, the trio crowded together in their portaledge—a tent that's anchored right into the rock wall. It seemed like the crisis had passed. They lit their propane stove and warmed up some couscous (sounds like COOS-coos) for dinner. The weather was clear, and they were able to finally breathe a little easier.

This sense of peace didn't last long, however. The next morning, a bar that stabilized the portaledge suddenly snapped—in a split second, the tent was dangling from a sheer granite wall!

"We're Himalayan big wall climbing, and we broke our portaledge," Jimmy said, emphasizing the final words as the shock set in.

After making sure everyone was safe, the team realized how big the problem was. The "ledge," as climbers call it, was a vital piece of equipment. Without it, they wouldn't have any shelter from the cold.

But mountaineers are always quick with a creative fix. Jimmy, Conrad, and Renan used ice screws and athletic tape to stabilize the broken bar and were soon ready to move on.

The next section of the expedition was "big wall climbing." In this style, one climber goes ahead to set the path—using special screws, hooks, and bolts to secure the ropes. It would take multiple days and require the team to camp in the portaledge along the route.

Jimmy started out in the lead, on a tricky pitch nicknamed House of Cards. It was a nearly vertical wall of granite, made up of huge blocks that are only held together with grit and ice. If one of these blocks were to fall, Jimmy would be ripped right off the mountain. Conrad and

Did You Know?

Climbers in the Himalaya have a deep respect for the local people's beliefs, often stringing up prayer flags meant to spread strength, peace, compassion, and wisdom to the surrounding countryside.

Renan would likely be pulled off with him.

It was one of the most dangerous and technical sections of the entire trip, and Jimmy took his time. He drew slow, even breaths of the icy mountain air and made sure he felt certain about each hand or foot placement.

"These giant blocks," he said, tapping the granite with a hammer secured to his belt loop, "they are moving under my weight."

As Jimmy set hooks along the House of Cards, his friends watched from below. No move was made without planning— even a second of lost focus could put the whole expedition at risk.

After six hours, the painstaking pitch was finally over. The team was closing in on the summit!

Jimmy Chin attempts to summit Shark's Fin.

Chapter 3

FINISHING THE FIN

For seven days on the mountain, Jimmy, Conrad, and Renan had the best weather they could hope for. It was cold, but they hadn't yet faced a serious storm. So far, the howling winds and snow that haunted their first attempt had missed them.

The night before they set out for the summit, the team's luck seemed to run out.

The wind tore across the nylon surface of the portaledge, and snow swirled around the tent.

After five or six hours, the snow showed no signs of stopping. Jimmy became very worried.

After all they'd been through, it looked like the weather might shut them down again. At such high altitudes, battling wind and snow would be one complication too many.

Near 1 a.m., as if to answer the wishes of the three battered climbers, the skies cleared. Jimmy peeked his head past the tent flaps and saw stars twinkling high above. It was

Did You Know?

Sleep is hard to come by on Shark's Fin. Jimmy's team would often start climbing in the middle of the night and all through the next day.

their chance. The friends geared up and started their race to the peak, braving the bone-chilling cold.

"It's probably negative twenty out," Jimmy said between swings of his ice axe, "and I can't feel my feet."

The next portion of the climb was mixed ice and rock, up a nearly vertical wall. Conrad led the way, charging for the summit. It was extremely technical climbing, and it had to be done quickly. Otherwise the team might get stuck rushing to the top of the mountain at sunset, 15 hours later.

Altitude Sickness

At higher altitudes, the air we breathe is thinner—that means that it has less oxygen molecules per square foot than air at lower elevations. With less oxygen getting to the brain and muscles, both systems can develop problems—as likely happened with Renan.

There's one surefire cure for altitude sickness: going to a lower altitude. But mountaineers can also acclimatize—meaning their bodies adjust, as Renan's did after he struggled with altitude on Shark's Fin. With time and luck, it's amazing how the human body can adjust to change.

The team finally arrived at the summit ridge. This is where they had turned around during the previous trip. Now they had the final unknown section left to climb.

Conrad, who was thought of as the head of the group, turned to Jimmy and offered him the chance to lead the final pitch. Jimmy shoved the handle of his ice axe in the snow and began to climb. As he jammed his crampons—sharp spikes that fit over climbing boots—into the ice and pulled himself up a few feet at a time, he knew: They were going to make it!

Jimmy's final move was to wrestle his way up two ledges of granite. Then he hugged the very tip of Shark's Fin.

"Wooooooooooooo!" Jimmy screamed, stretching his arms wide

and smiling down at his friends. His face glowed. "Woooooohooooo!"

Conrad and Renan followed him up, and the three of them shared high fives, hugs, and tears of joy. Their hard work had paid off. They had climbed Meru. More importantly, they'd pushed their own limits and seized a dream that had often seemed out of reach.

As they gazed across the entire Garhwal Himalayas, the clouds shifted below them and the enormity of their accomplishment set in. They were the first three people *ever* to summit the Shark's Fin route. They would go down in the record books as the team that conquered an "impossible" climb.

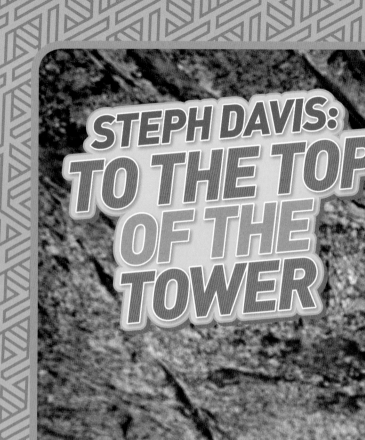

STEPH DAVIS: TO THE TOP OF THE TOWER

Steph Davis is an expert free climber, which means she climbs rocks without ropes!

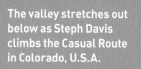

The valley stretches out below as Steph Davis climbs the Casual Route in Colorado, U.S.A.

Chapter 1

THE DIAMOND ON LONGS PEAK

On a warm day in September, the air was still crisp and fresh up where Steph Davis hung on to a rock wall. She drew steady breaths and thought about her every move. She was climbing the Casual Route on the eastern face of Longs Peak, a mountain summit more than 14,000 feet (4,267 m) high in the Rocky Mountains. The valley floor stretched out below her.

Stretching for a hold, Steph was struck by a powerful emotion. It made her heart race and her lungs feel tight. It was fear, and it came over her as she stood with her feet wide apart and one hand jammed into a narrow crack in the rock face.

"I thought I'd prepared myself," Steph said, "but I suddenly felt really intimidated, really scared. The rock face was kind of slippery and not really secure."

Steph didn't like feeling overwhelmed by fear. It meant that there was a problem, and in the sort of climbing that she does, even the littlest problem can mean the difference between life and death. That's because Steph doesn't use a rope or pound bolts into the granite. Her only tools are her mind, body, and years of experience.

Did You Know?

Steph uses positive self-talk to keep her spirits up during climbs. Maybe it would work for you, the next time you feel challenged!

This type of climbing is called free soloing. It is done without any gear (usually after practicing the same route *with* gear), and it's for experts only. Even then, they only climb routes that they're sure they can handle.

"If you get scared in the middle of a long free solo," Steph said, "you've made a mistake in being there."

There weren't any easy solutions for the situation Steph found herself in on Longs Peak. She was alone with the rock hundreds of feet off the ground.

"It was terrible," Steph said. "I was climbing for my life. There was no way out."

After a moment of hesitation, Steph did the only thing she could do: She kept moving. She climbed past the route's crux, quickly and nervously. As she searched for new holds, she regained focus.

Soon, Steph arrived at a more comfortable section—a crack in the rock face. The crack allowed Steph to jam her hand into the narrow gap and then make a fist, in order to have a solid anchor point. With one hand locked in, a crack climber feels more comfortable searching for the next hold or finding a new foot position.

Once Steph got back into a groove, she felt better immediately. Her fear passed, and soon she was standing on the summit. By sending—short for ascending in rock climber talk—the Casual Route, Steph had become the first woman to free

solo the Diamond,
a giant wall on
Longs Peak.

Instead of being
thrilled over this tremendous
accomplishment, Steph felt
frustrated. She was angry that fear had
gotten the better of her, even for a moment.

"From the outside you look and you say
'Oh, look, she did it!'" Steph explained.
"But I did *not* have the fear-free experience
I was trying to have."

For many climbers, the next step would
be to leave Longs Peak behind for a while—
to climb other rock faces or explore new
routes. But not Steph. Her goal is to feel
comfortable and confident while free soloing;
simply making it to the top isn't enough.

Some Climbing Holds

BUCKETS: These holds are like grabbing the rim of a bucket. They're easy to grip and give climbers a feeling of security.

CRIMPS: These tiny edges on the rock face don't feel very secure at all. Climbers have to grip them with their fingertips!

FINGER CRACKS: There are many types of holds in crack climbing. Sometimes the route follows a narrow crack with only enough space for two fingers!

LEDGES: These flat rock ledges offer no rim to grab, but climbers still feel safer than they do with a crimp.

Rather than heading back to Yosemite (sounds like yo-SEM-ih-tee), California, U.S.A., where she'd first become famous, or Moab (sounds like MOW-ab), Utah, U.S.A., where she now lives, Steph stayed in Colorado. After free soloing a route called the Flying Buttress, she felt ready to approach the Casual Route again.

The second time around, Steph finished the route without any feelings of fear or panic. But she still wasn't ready to leave. Instead, she decided to climb the Diamond a third time—free soloing an even tougher line to the top called Pervertical Sanctuary.

On the morning of the climb, Steph woke up at 3:30 a.m., long before the sun peeked over the horizon. Right away, she felt like she had a better sense of focus, thanks to her experiences on the Casual Route. She had a plan and a positive attitude, which are key for any free solo climber.

The crux of Pervertical Sanctuary is made of finger cracks. This means that instead of being able to jam her whole hand in the crack, Steph would only be able to fit a few fingers. With the morning sun poking through the clouds and warming her up, Steph reminded herself that crack climbing is her specialty. She concentrated on getting solid finger holds, good foot locks, and remaining calm.

Even in the most dangerous section, where she was literally clinging to the rock by her fingertips, Steph didn't feel the same overwhelming fear she had on the

Casual Route. She breathed steadily through every move—completely in the moment and confident in her skills.

With that climb, Steph became the first woman, and the second person ever, to free solo Pervertical Sanctuary. It was a remarkable accomplishment. And how did she celebrate? She climbed it again!

"This is about having the experience I want to have," Steph said. "Not just surviving."

The second climb was a success, too. Steph finally felt fully satisfied. Not only had she become the first woman ever to free solo the Diamond, she'd done it four times on two different routes in one summer!

It was time to leave Longs Peak and decide on her next big climbing project.

Castleton Tower is a 400-foot (120-m) sandstone tower in Castle Valley, Utah.

Chapter 2

CASTLETON TOWER

Less than a year after her four climbs on the Diamond, Steph stood atop Castleton Tower, a massive rock pillar jutting from the ground in Utah's Castle Valley. From this spot, she had a stunning view of the red valley floor below her. She could see similar towers in the distance, more than a mile away. She drew long breaths and marveled at the beautiful landscape.

After a few minutes, Steph took off her backpack and set it down. She covered it with stones to keep it in place. On this trip, she'd summited with ropes—like a traditional sport climb—but the next time she climbed the tower, she would be attempting its first ever free solo ascent by a woman.

If everything went according to plan, Steph would be back to this same spot just a few days later with no gear at all, and she would *need* that backpack. It held the key to her descent back to the base of the tower. But before seeing the backpack again, Steph would have to complete the toughest free solo climb of her life.

To prepare for this difficult project, Steph planned out every last detail. She checked and double-checked the weather forecast. Many of the world's best climbing spots have warm weather during the summer months, but climbing in the heat isn't ideal—sweaty hands are a climber's worst enemy.

"I needed a day where I felt good to go," Steph explained. "I wanted the perfect climbing temperature and no wind."

A few days after dropping her backpack off at the top of Castleton Tower, Steph woke up to the exact morning she'd been waiting for. The conditions were just right, and she knew how she wanted to approach the climb. Similar with the Diamond, the key to her plan was the need to feel in control.

> **Did You Know?**
>
> Castleton Tower is one of the most popular climbs in America— with various routes to the top on all of the tower's sides. It was first summited in 1961.

"There's a level of preparation that is required to do something so hard," she said. "You can't really shortcut the work of things."

For Steph's free solo climb at Castleton Tower, she'd have to use the skills she'd learned across her entire career, but particularly on her four ascents on the Diamond. She'd also been climbing the tower route with ropes and other gear to collect beta—information about which moves she'd need on her route.

"When I'm climbing the route with gear to prepare," she explained, "I'm basically identifying the hard sections and making sure I know exactly what I'm going to do in those places when I don't have gear."

Turn Down the Heat!

Extreme heat, and avoiding sweaty hands, is a big deal for boulderers and sport climbers. That's why you'll always see them with chalk on their hands to prevent slipping.

Another reason climbers don't want it too hot is the rubber on their climbing shoes. In cool conditions, it molds to the rock and grips it. Once the temperatures start to climb, the rubber becomes too soft. An amateur (sounds like AM-uh-tur) might not notice this change, but a pro would. And a free soloist—paying attention to every tiny detail—*definitely* would.

Steph found
that her route was
easily divided into
three parts. After
each stretch, she'd
be able to take a little
break and regroup.
Each section had easier
chunks and a crux of its own. The
third crux would be the most difficult—
almost like a video game, with the hardest
level at the end.

Before starting her climb, Steph looked
up at the tower, drew deep breaths, and
dusted her hands with chalk. The first
100 feet (30 m) of the climb allowed her
to warm up and get in a rhythm. She was
able to mentally prepare for the first

crux—an exposed section with unclear foot placement.

"You still have a crack, but you're not really climbing *in* the crack," Steph said, explaining this crux. "You're just pressing your feet on the slippery coating on the rock while your hands are grabbing the crack."

Without a rope, that sort of exposure can be terrifying—the climber has no sense of security. Steph reminded herself that her climbing shoes would stick on the rock, even though it was slick. She used positive phrases to help herself feel comfortable. Still, she found herself gripping the rock a little too hard.

"When you don't have a rope, sometimes you hold on harder than you should," Steph said. "It's this constant battle of trying to not hold on too hard and get tired, but still holding on hard enough that you feel like you're not going to just pop off."

Even with all of her preparation, she knew that there would be little glitches. No climb is the same every time. The key for a free solo climber is how you respond when something unexpected happens. Do you remain calm, or do you panic?

"I was actually a little cold that day, so I had my pants unrolled," said Steph, recalling a frightening moment from that first crux. "As I was moving my feet, I actually stepped on my pant leg and it made my foot slip."

Without ropes, something as small as stepping on a pant leg is a huge deal.

It would be easy for a climber to lose her cool.

"I had to really clamp down with my hands to save myself," Steph said. "You try to predict everything, but you just can't."

That moment got her heart racing, but Steph never let fear get the best of her. She handled it smoothly—recovering her footing quickly. Seconds later, she was moving again.

Soon, Steph had finished the first section of the tower. There was a rock ledge, and she scrambled up onto it and then sat down with her back against the cool stone. Two more sections to go!

Steph Davis prepared to free solo Castleton Tower by first climbing it with gear.

Chapter 3

A SUMMIT SURPRISE

After the first section of the climb, Steph sat on the rock ledge and breathed. She needed a break after feeling like she'd gripped the rock face a little too hard during the first crux and to regroup from slipping on her pant leg.

"You can't just sit there and think about the past," she explained. "You just have to move on and say, 'Okay, forget about that.'"

After taking a few more slow and steady breaths, Steph knew it was time to move on. There was a backpack waiting for her at the top of the tower.

The crux of the second section actually started right off the ledge. Steph was excited about this—she would get through it and have the chance to cruise to the second platform. She'd need the rest, because the third part of the climb was by far the hardest.

"Right off the first ledge there's a steep, angling, diagonal crack," Steph said. "It's hard to be straight on your feet, because you're going up and sideways."

Making her way up this stretch, Steph felt like she was in a groove—locked in and secure. Soon, she was on the second ledge.

She didn't need to dwell on this section of the climb because it had gone as smoothly as she could have hoped. Instead, she used all her mental energy to prepare for the third section.

"Doing the third part without a rope really intimidated me," Steph said. "It's a crack, but there's a part where it overhangs, so you can't just be standing on your feet."

When a rock wall overhangs, it means that the wall has gone beyond vertical and hangs above her. In this third crux section, not only did the wall overhang, but there was a place where Steph would have to leave the crack altogether.

As she gathered herself for the crux moves, Steph reminded herself not to panic without the security of the crack. She knew that it would just be a few hard pulls. She kept her breathing steady; she felt sure she could handle it. Now, it was just a matter of making the moves she'd practiced. There was no room for error!

"I couldn't afford to have something like what happened in the first pitch, where my foot slipped," Steph said. "You have to grab this rounded hold, pull up on it, and throw your feet up higher. I'm thinking, If something crazy happens and my feet kick off, it's going to be a lot harder to hold on. It's complete and total commitment."

Steph made the move without a mistake. She got over the overhang and rocked back up into the crack. The wall was vertical again—Steph had made it through the third crux.

For the rest of the climb, the crack widened. Soon, Steph's whole body was in the crack. She finished the final section with a scramble up small ledges to a flat plateau (sounds like plat-OH) at the top. She'd done it. She'd become the first person to ever free solo the North Face of Castleton Tower!

With the climb complete, Steph let herself relax for a moment. Sure, there was still the matter of getting down, but that would be the fun part. It was time to take in the scenery, to calm down, and to collect her backpack.

BASE Jumping

The backpack Steph left at the top of Castleton Tower was a BASE jumping parachute. BASE stands for building, antenna (human-made towers), span (bridges), and earth (cliffs)—the four objects that participants in the sport like to jump from. But the truth is that Steph is only interested in jumping off cliffs.

A BASE jumping parachute looks like a skydiving parachute, but it's made to open much quicker. Just like free solo climbing, BASE jumping is for experts only. Most BASE jumpers recommend you not even start training until you've logged at least 300 skydives!

"Free soloing requires this pretty extreme level of focus," Steph said. "So when it's finished, you can stop and say, 'Okay, I'm safe now.'"

After a short break, Steph crossed the top of the tower and tossed the rocks off of her backpack. She checked it over and then slipped it over her shoulders and fastened it in place with a cross strap. It had been three days since she'd left the backpack on the top of the tower, and now she was finally ready to use it.

Once again, Steph drew a deep breath of crisp morning air. She reminded herself that she knew what she was doing, that she was trained and prepared. Next, she stepped to the edge of Castleton Tower and leapt into the air!

For two seconds, Steph was stretched out, free-falling through space, wind tearing against her. Then she reached behind her, grabbed the bottom of the backpack, and released what's called a pilot chute. The pilot chute created enough drag to pull out a full parachute. As it billowed out, Steph knew her adventure was almost over.

Three minutes later, Steph was standing on the red sand of Castle Valley. She'd completed the most difficult free solo of her life and BASE jumped off the top of Castleton Tower. She'd also pushed past the fear she'd felt back on the Diamond in Colorado, completing the climb in just the way she'd wanted—calm, confident, and in control.

THE END

DON'T MISS!

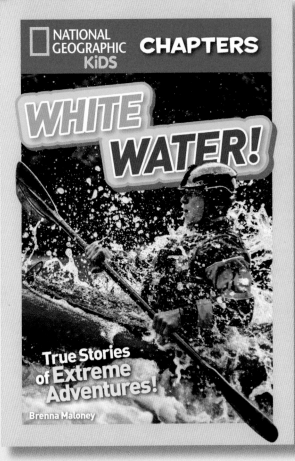

NATIONAL GEOGRAPHIC KiDS **CHAPTERS**

WHITE WATER!

True Stories of Extreme Adventures!

Brenna Maloney

Turn the page for a sneak preview . . .

Todd Wells is followed by two of his teammates as they explore the Chitina River.

RIVER OF RISK

The team rests in a patch of cottongrass after scouting the first portion of the Headwaters Canyon.

Chapter 1

SCOUTING THE RIVER

Alaska, U.S.A.

Todd Wells was wide-awake. Around him, his teammates snored and mumbled in their sleep. But not Todd. As expedition leader, he had too much on his mind. He had led other expeditions before, but none like this one. Todd and his five teammates were about to try something that no one had ever done before. And it was risky.

Todd's group was camped in the heart of the Wrangell (sounds like RANG-guhl) Mountains. Their tents were nestled in one of Alaska's most breathtaking valleys. But they weren't here to camp. They were here to run the Chitina (CHIT-nuh) River.

"Running" the river means traveling down it in kayaks (sounds like KY-yaks). All six team members were experienced kayakers. Yet this 130-mile (209-km)-long river is unique.

Lower parts of the Chitina River are a favorite among boaters, who take to the river in kayaks, rafts, canoes, and other small boats. But one section of the river had never been run. That's because until recently, this section was covered in ice.

The source of the river—called the headwaters—comes from the towering Logan Glacier (sounds like GLAY-shur). This massive block of ice flows into the river from the east. The Chugach (sounds like CHOO-gach) Mountains lie to the south. The Wrangells are to the north. A deep canyon cuts between these ranges, and the Chitina runs through the canyon. The first 10 miles (16 km) of the river have always been frozen and impassable.

Over time, changes in the climate have brought about warmer temperatures. The Logan Glacier has been slowly but steadily melting. As a result, this ice has become turbulent (sounds like TUR-byuh-lent), fast-moving water. Is it passable? That's what Todd and his team had come to discover.

For more than a year, the team had been planning this expedition. They had pored over topographic (sounds like top-uh-GRAF-ik) maps and satellite (sounds like SAT-uh-lite) images of the river. They had talked to local people who had grown up in the area and knew the river well. They talked to other kayakers and boaters who had paddled the lower sections of the river. They had done their homework. But now that they were here, Todd knew he needed to read the river with his own eyes. The best way to do that was from the sky.

After his restless night, Todd asked a local bush pilot to take him up in his small plane. The plane lifted off from a runway in McCarthy, an end-of-the-road town in the Wrangell–St. Elias National Park.

It easily carried
them above the
Logan Glacier and
over the Headwaters
Canyon. For the first
time, Todd could see clearly
what they had been studying.
But he wasn't ready for what he saw.

It wasn't like looking at a map or a
photo. This river moved. A lot. The gray,
murky water churned. To Todd, it seemed
like a living, breathing beast.

The scale of the river overwhelmed
him. It was massive. In the photos, some
features had looked small and easy. In real
life, they were very different. He saw
waves towering 10 feet (3 m) high or taller.
There were deadly pour-overs, where

shallow water moved quickly over partially submerged (sounds like suhb-MURJD) rocks. From upstream, these looked like big, rounded waves. But Todd knew that once a paddler got over one, he could get caught in the swirling water.

The pilot flew over the river several times so that Todd could make sense of what he was seeing. The sheer volume of water worried Todd. It was early August and unusually hot. All that heat was causing more glacier melt, which was raising the levels of the river. *Too much melt,* Todd thought. *The conditions aren't good. They aren't safe.*

The pilot flew on. There was a specific point in the river he wanted Todd to see. It was a rapid they called "the Pinch."

The Logan Glacier

Glaciers are huge masses of ice that "flow" like very slow rivers. They form over hundreds of years where fallen snow compresses (sounds like kuhm-PRESS-ez) and turns into ice. Glaciers form the largest reservoir (sounds like REZ-er-vwahr) of freshwater on the planet. In fact, they store 75 percent of the world's freshwater! Warmer weather has led to faster melting of the Logan Glacier...

Want to know what happens next? Be sure to check out *White Water!* Available wherever books and ebooks are sold.

INDEX

MORE INFORMATION

A note for parents and teachers: For more information about the climbers featured in this book, you can visit these websites with your young readers.

To follow Ashima Shiraishi, check out her Instagram page:
instagram.com/ ashimashiraishi

To follow Jimmy Chin, check out his website and Instagram page:
jimmychin.com
instagram.com/jimmychin

To follow Steph Davis, check out her website and Instagram page:
stephdavis.co
instagram.com/highsteph

CREDITS

For Nikta—rock climber, adventure partner, and first reader all in one! —SB

ACKNOWLEDGMENTS

Special thanks to Jimmy Chin, Ashima Shiraishi, and Steph Davis for sharing their stories; my friends and family, who are always so patient with a writer under deadline; and true rock star editors Shelby Alinsky and Souzanne Plasse—teamwork made the dream work! Thanks, too, to the other incredible members of the book team: Kathryn Williams, Christina Ascani, and Sanjida Rashid.